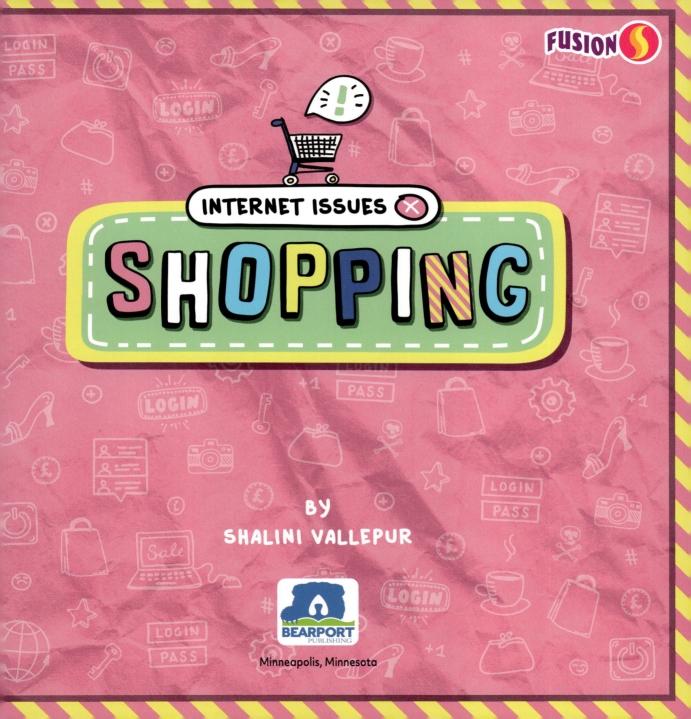

Credits
All images are courtesy of Shutterstock.com, unless otherwise specified. With thanks to Getty Images, Thinkstock Photo, and iStockphoto. Front Cover – Bloomicon, Alex Gontar, George Rudy, New Africa, Twin Design. Images used on every page – Bloomicon, Alex Gontar. 2 – Bloomicon. 4–5 – Aquarius Studio, George Rudy, Monkey Business Images. 6–7 – Andrey_Popov, aslysun, Monkey Business Images. 8–9 – Dragon Images, LightField Studios, McLittle Stock, Mr_Mrs_Marcha, Worawee Meepian. 10–11 – Kaspars Grinvalds, Rawpixel.com, Tomek_Pa. 12–13 – EugeneEdge, Rawpixel.com, Sam72. 14–15 – Andrew Rybalko, BoxerX, SynthEx. 16–17 – McLittle Stock, Sam72, solarseven. 18–19 – fizkes, New Afric, _shutterstock. 20–21 – fizkes, Iurii Stepanov, Rawpixel.com. 22–23 – Dragon Images, Sarawut Chainawara.

Bearport Publishing Company Product Development Team
President: Jen Jenson; Director of Product Development: Spencer Brinker; Managing Editor: Allison Juda; Associate Editor: Naomi Reich; Associate Editor: Tiana Tran; Senior Designer: Colin O'Dea; Associate Designer: Elena Klinkner; Associate Designer: Kayla Eggert; Product Development Specialist: Anita Stasson

Library of Congress Cataloging-in-Publication Data

Names: Vallepur, Shalini, author.
Title: Shopping / Shalini Vallepur.
Description: Fusion books. | Minneapolis : Bearport Publishing Company, 2023. | Series: Internet issues | Includes index.
Identifiers: LCCN 2023009178 (print) | LCCN 2023009179 (ebook) | ISBN 9798885099615 (library binding) | ISBN 9798888221372 (paperback) | ISBN 9798888222812 (ebook)
Subjects: LCSH: Teleshopping--Juvenile literature. | Internet--Safety measures--Juvenile literature.
Classification: LCC TX335.5 .V35 2023 (print) | LCC TX335.5 (ebook) | DDC 381/.142--dc23/eng/20230301
LC record available at https://lccn.loc.gov/2023009178
LC ebook record available at https://lccn.loc.gov/2023009179

© 2024 BookLife Publishing
This edition is published by arrangement with BookLife Publishing.

North American adaptations © 2024 Bearport Publishing Company. All rights reserved. No part of this publication may be reproduced in whole or in part, stored in any retrieval system, or transmitted in any form or by any means, electronic, mechanical, photocopying, recording, or otherwise, without written permission from the publisher.

For more information, write to Bearport Publishing, 5357 Penn Avenue South, Minneapolis, MN 55419.

CONTENTS

The Internet 4
Shopping Online 6
Personal Information 10
Scams 12
Spotting Scams 14
Pop-ups 16
Different Devices 18
Safe and Secure 20
All You Need to Know 22
Glossary 24
Index 24

THE INTERNET

Have you been on the internet? It connects computers, smartphones, and other **devices** all around the world.

People use the internet every day. They use it for work, to learn, to buy things, and even to talk with other people.

SHOPPING ONLINE

ONLINE SHOPPING

Many people use the internet to buy things. This is called online shopping.

Online means on the internet.

ONLINE SHOPPING IS FOR GROWN-UPS.

Things that are bought online need to be paid for, just like things bought in a store.

Some stores have their own websites or **apps**. You can buy things from these online spaces to be sent straight to your home.

YOU CAN BUY FOOD ONLINE FROM GROCERY STORE WEBSITES.

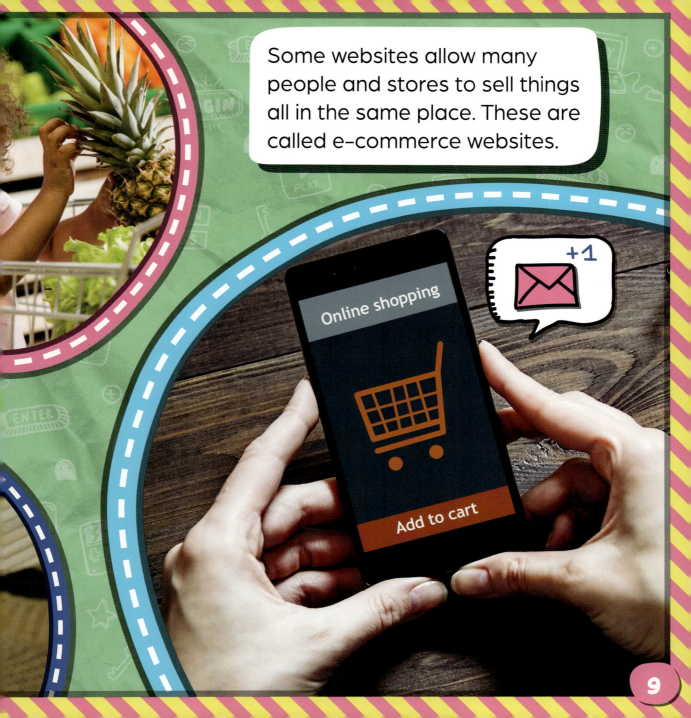

Some websites allow many people and stores to sell things all in the same place. These are called e-commerce websites.

PERSONAL INFORMATION

To shop online, you usually need to make an **account**. This often means sharing personal information, such as your full name and address.

EMAIL ADDRESS

USERNAME

PASSWORD

BE CAREFUL WHO YOU GIVE YOUR PERSONAL INFORMATION TO ONLINE.

FULL NAME

ADDRESS

10

USUALLY, AN ADULT NEEDS TO SHARE BANK OR CREDIT CARD INFORMATION TO BUY THINGS ONLINE.

Be sure you trust the websites you are shopping from online. Sharing information with online stores you do not trust is risky.

SCAMS

Scams are tricks. They can get you to share your personal information online.

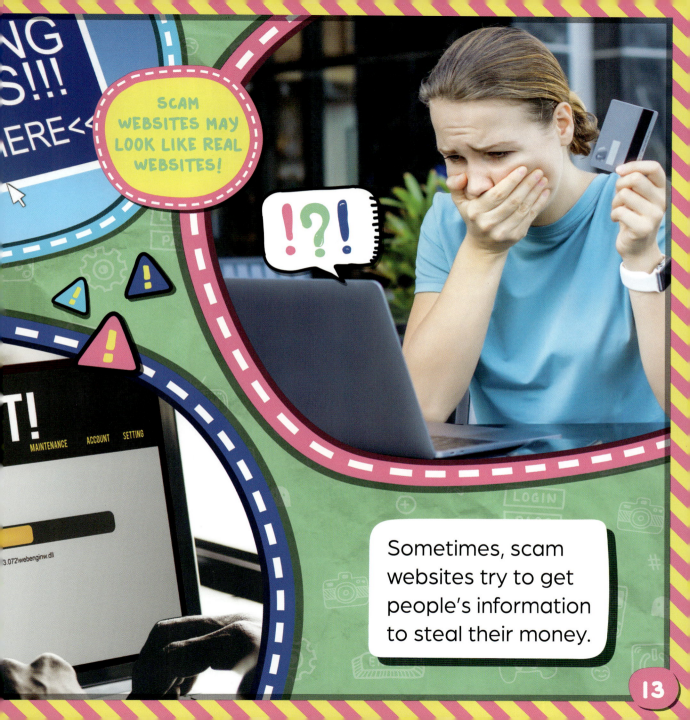

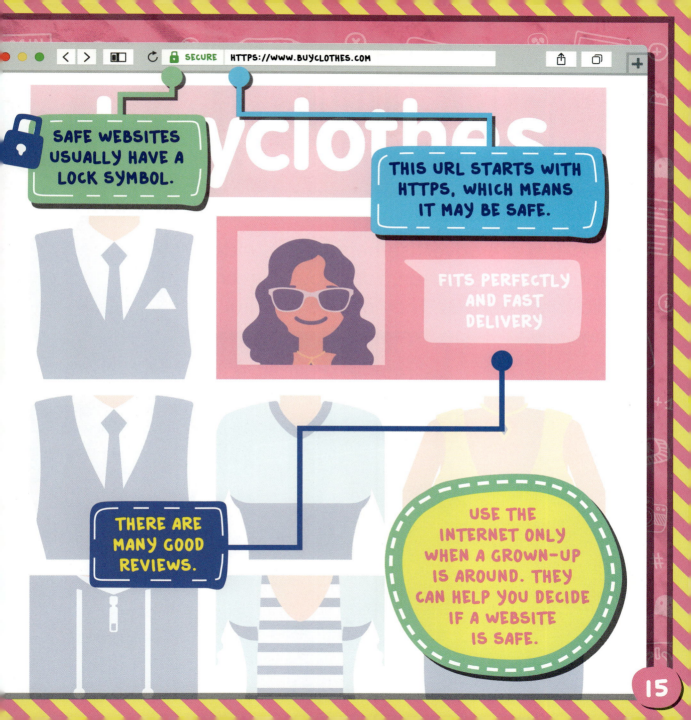

POP-UPS

Pop-ups are advertisements that suddenly appear on the screen. You should never click on a pop-up. They can be harmful.

SOME POP-UPS MAY GIVE YOUR DEVICE A **VIRUS**.

DIFFERENT DEVICES

Some people save their bank information on their devices. This makes online shopping faster. But it can mean you may buy something by mistake.

DON'T PANIC IF YOU BUY SOMETHING BY ACCIDENT. TELL A GROWN-UP RIGHT AWAY.

Be careful when using someone else's device. It can be easy to buy something when you do not mean to.

SAFE AND SECURE

Online shopping can be helpful and easy. However, it's important to look out for scams, pop-ups, and viruses. Most devices have security programs to help stop these things.

WARNING! VIRUS DETECTED!

A grown-up can make sure a device has its security settings turned on.

ALL YOU NEED TO KNOW

Now you know about online shopping. Let's review some of the things we have learned.

POP-UPS CAN LEAD TO SCAMS OR VIRUSES.

SECURITY PROGRAMS HELP KEEP OUR DEVICES SAFE.

A SAFE URL STARTS WITH HTTPS AND HAS A LOCK SYMBOL.

GLOSSARY

accidentally happening by mistake

account a login for a website that connects with your personal information

advertisements posters, videos, or pictures that tell about things that are for sale

apps things on phones or tablets that do different tasks

devices machines such as tablets, smartphones, and computers

reviews comments about a product, service, or experience that talk about whether it is good or not

scam something that tricks people, usually for money

URL the address for a webpage

virus a harmful program that deletes or steals information

INDEX

accounts 10
bank information 11, 18
e-commerce 9
personal information 10–13, 17, 23

pop-ups 14, 16–17, 20, 22
scams 12–14, 20, 22–23

security 20–22
URL 14–15, 22
viruses 16, 20, 22
websites 8–9, 11, 13–15